CHUM KIU: WING CHUN'S ART OF WAR

JASON KOROL

MARTIAL WAY PRESS

To the great Wing Chun students out there who I haven't met nor personally trained with. Your support, as well as your dedication to this great art we both love, is forever humbling.

"There's no such thing as life without bloodshed. I think the notion that the species can be improved in some way, that everyone could live in harmony, is a really dangerous idea. Those who are afflicted with this notion are the first ones to give up their souls, their freedom. Your desire that it be that way will enslave you and make your life vacuous."
    Cormac McCarthy

1

AN APOLOGY

The author is terribly regretful for the fact that you're left with him as the model doing the form. Our attempt to hire Margot Robbie failed miserably. She never responded to any of our emails or entreaties. In fact, there may now even be some kind of restraining order. A court case may or may not be pending.

Bummer, that.

We also tried to have a few nice pictures of puppies to break up all the violence but that didn't pan out either as the little cutie wasn't house-trained. It kept peeing on our Mook Jong.

Lesson learned.

Nevertheless, always chipper and not one to dwell on defeat, the author has, in fact, gotten a haircut as well as a new outfit since his last Wing Chun book.

But no Margot and no puppy.

Maybe in the Biu Jee book we'll get all that straightened out. Sorry.

2

THE FORM

*The basic start position. Take a deep breath and slow your thoughts
down so you can focus. Don't race past this position as it should
serve as an emotional, intellectual and physical check. Let go of any
tension in the muscles and/or mind. This position is the most
important in the form (INDEED!) because it serves as an instructor
so that we become self-aware of tension of mind and body.*

Simultaneously bring your hands up to the Sout Kuen (chambered fist) position while bending the knees. Be mindful to keep the your feet fully on the floor as your knees sink. This bent knee position serves as your reference for how much your knees should be bent when fighting. If you have to change your foot position or can't keep your entire foot on the floor, you've bent too far.

Push your toes out while remaining balanced.

To pull your heels out, have your toes grip the floor and then lock into your basic stance. Your hips should be pressed slightly forward and the energy between the knees should be pressing inward. Some people really overdo this aspect and use a pigeon-toed stance. Some also combine this with a pronounced backward lean. We think that's too much of a good thing...like taking too many vitamins. The idea is to develop good body feel as a foundation for the footwork and shifting to come. This stance, the SLT Ma, isn't an end in and of itself. It's the foundation upon which we build. The purpose of it is to serve as a launching pad, not as a ball and chain.

Like with the first form, SLT, the elbows push the hands forward so that they cross low in front of the centerline. The belly button is right about the low edge. Going lower than this with hand techniques is discouraged as it's not structurally efficient.

The hands circle underneath/back toward the body and then grab from the top position. In another way of saying it, they curl underneath and then end up in this top position.

Return back to the basic stance - Yi Ji Kim Yeung Ma (YJKYM), also known as the character two goat-gripping stance.

Use your elbow to drive your fist to the center position in preparation for the basic straight punch. Stay relaxed and be prepared to snappily but smoothly punch down the center line.

The basic straight punch, or Jeet Kuen, is the workhorse of our offensive/defensive arsenal. Stay loose while driving the punch forward and then the wrist and forearm should snap into a locked position at extension. Never go to full extension. The elbow should not lock out. After the punch, relax the arm without dropping it.

Open your hand into a tan-sao position.

As in the SLT form, rotate your left hand clockwise without moving your elbow. This is called Huen Sao or Circling Hand.

When your Huen-Sao has completed its motion, close your hand quickly as if grabbing something. This repeated action is preparing you not just for Lop-Sao (coming next) but Chin-Na too. There's a lot of grabbing, pulling, locking and breaking in Wing Chun which we'll explore later. Get ready for all that by practicing these actions correctly.

Pull your closed hand back to the Sout Kuen position. This is both a Lop-Sao (pulling hand) action and a backward elbow strike. This action should be done with snappy looseness in the Chum Kiu form. Economical power is the result of right practice.

Repeat the Jeet Kuen actions now on the right side.

*The straight punch shouldn't be taken for granted. Proper punching with the bottom three knuckles, thrown with structure and snap, is the mark of the expert. Without discipline, we'll swing rather than punch - thereby telegraphing our blow, swinging inaccurately, landing with the wrong part of our fist, and losing our balance. As always, what seems so obvious in life isn't. Wing Chun is **fistic wisdom**. Follow its tenets, practice them, think about them carefully, and you'll be free from the tyranny of having to learn only from experience.*

Open your hand into the Tan-Sao position. Stay relaxed and snappy with your movements. Be careful not to let your chambered hand start to droop or your shoulders turn. In other words, stay vigilant yet relaxed.

Use the Huen-Sao counter clockwise.

Grab and use the Lop-Sao. This action and truth should encourage all Wing Chun students to work on their grip strength outside of class. Reverse curls at the gym and chin-ups are great ways to improve your forearm and wrist strength.

As always, we return back to our foundational base. Not having a base is like not having a standard. This invites chaos into our lives and actions. Far from being a simply arbitrary position, the YJKYM in Wing Chun provides us a practical and theoretical center for our training. It reminds us that balance and discipline are central components to success.

Thus concludes the opening of Chum Kiu. Now we move on to the first of three major sections called the *Yiu Ma* section. Yiu Ma basically means waist energy from the shifting of the YJKYM structure. Not that I didn't say the shifting of the YJKYM itself but the structure of it. There's a subtle difference at work. In Wing Chun forms we should always remember that all of the actions are principles in motion. We learn how to both diffuse energy through shifting when needed and how to gain power through the coordinated actions of the body's power line.

Double Jum Sao (sinking elbow) is executed by bringing the elbows into the middle.

The hands drive forward towards the center-mass and nerve center of the enemy, which is his neck, throat, jaw, eyes and head. There isn't a particular tool attached to this movement (like an eye-gouge). The point is the structure. The necessary weapon can be attached as needed. We remind the reader that Wing Chun is a self-defense system that attacks and defends the body's weakest targets. Don't forget that about this action. It's the crux of infighting.

The hands drop loosely into the double Lan-Sao (bar arm) position. Left is over the right. The arms shouldn't be any higher than the lower chest so as to develop good muscle memory and balance.

Here's the first shift. Without winding up or bouncing to get momentum, shift to 45 degrees to your left. The big idea is to teach us how to move our structure as a unit - knees, hips, shoulders and elbows. Novices, to get power, resort to crude actions like swings. The Wing Chun fighter learns to deliver maximum power without the extremes of telegraphing and overcommitment.

This second shift is often a little easier than the first. While again not using any sort of wind-up, shift to the right. Stop at 45 degrees again. The power line of knees, hips, shoulders and elbows are trained to act as a unit.

Shift back, careful to keep the pressure in your stance. Think about it as using your right knee to press your left toe. This will keep you rooted and yet mobile. Shifting should be trained slowly so as to avoid technical error. Your balance should be kept on the front of the heels...not leaning back too far as that's "too much of a good thing".

Open your guard by dropping the elbows, which fires the hands forward. This brings us to a position similar to the famous Muay Thai guard and is quite a useful position for fighting.

The elbows slightly press the elbows forward as the hands rotate outward to a palm-up position. Do not overextend. Stay balanced and springy. This tan-sao position isn't intended to pick off haymakers, incidentally. The previous, palms forward, is a stronger action. Pressing and pulling are stronger than adduction and abduction actions. Nevertheless, this action is a nifty "pick-off" or parry at longer distance when applicable. Furthermore, it allows us to "spread" force when on the inside or in a clinch.

Two-way energy is used as the left palm fires forward and upward and the right hand slaps backward to the left bicep. The motion should be powered by the elbow. Do not, repeat, do not simply move your hands and forget the structural lessons to be learned.

Repeat the cross-slap and palm action on the other side.

There's no contract signed in Wing Chun where you have to use any action exactly the way it appears in the form. You can use the backward slap solo just like you can the upward palm. That said, together they form a wonderful attack on the enemy's elbow should he leave his arm extended. Too often we assume Wing Chun is merely a close-quarter striking system when, in fact, it's a control method that includes striking, locking, pushing, pulling and, in this case, breaking.

The right palm is driven by the elbow to the left shoulder line while the left hand assumes the wu-sao (guarding hand) position.

As always, this is a type of action. The left vertical palm now fires to the right shoulder line. You'll notice that if you go past the shoulder line with the opposite hand that you lose considerable power in the action. Furthermore, you'll lose balance and recovery time.

This cycle of three vertical palms provides us the concept of range and power in our striking lines. The Wing Chun punch isn't limited to the direct centerline as this shows. Power and range are added when we use our structure to its fullest potential. If you throw a right hand punch, the left shoulder line is the structural limit to its capacity and vice versa. Wing Chun students often miss this lesson from Chum Kiu and illogically limit their punches.

Shift to the right by "connecting" your elbow and hip. Again, we're training unit power. We're training to "throw our weight around" without loss of balance. This is a seed technique for an elbow strike, yes, but it's much more than that. It's the training of proper shifting mechanics, which is more important than any one technique.

Shift to the bong-wu position. The wu-sao is in the same position it's in during SLT except that your body has shifted to the diagonal-on stance.

Shift again into the lan-sao position. Focus on fluidity and the elbow moving with the shift. This will greatly enhance your ability to use maximum power at short distance.

Back to bong-wu. Though the bong is important, we note that the elbow rises to the bong because the hip is shifting. This is teaching us the basis of what Dempsey called "upward surge" power. Again, the key to understanding the technique is that it's all about unit integration. Economical movements make us functionally faster and unit cohesion gives us maximum power. Without speed and power, we can't defend ourselves.

The shifting hip "pulls" the lan-sao elbow slightly downward. Thus, the shift teaches us how the upper body and lower body are connected in movement. That's the big idea here. Yes, we use the bong and wu for other things. But we won't use them to their maximum capacity if we miss the point.

Third shift back to bong-wu.

Shift back to lan-sao and chambered fist position.

Your elbow brings your punch to the launch point on the lan-sao.

Pull and hit. The lan-sao hands pulls back to the chambered position in a lop-sao grab as the punch fires. Two-way energy is developed. Practice this slowly and smoothly as it's easy to lose your balance.

Shift back to the forward facing position and draw your elbow back for a fak-sao (whipping/neck killing hand).

Complete the fak-sao.

Draw your elbow back to center using jum-sao (sinking elbow).

Just as with the end of SLT, but at mid-level, use your elbow energy to both push and pull, driving the left back and the right forward. Two-way energy without tension or loss of balance will enable you later to capture and destroy your enemy's limbs, so don't overlook this seemingly innocent action.

Huen-sao.

Back to the YJKYM.

Now we're going to repeat the previous section from the other side. Everything will be exactly the same except we're doing it in reverse.

Like last time, both hands, driven by the elbows, shoot forward. We can't be reminded enough to attack and defend "the nerve center" of the head and neck.

Drop your hands loosely back to double lan-sao, this time with your right on top. I always take a second and prepare for the shift, mindful to avoid bouncing to gain momentum.

Shift to the right. Stay focused on being relaxed throughout the movements. We're aiming at maximum speed and power down the road...we get there by logical integration of the structural elements.

Stay loose and smoothly shift to the left. Your weight should slightly to the right leg as you reach the end of the motion but not so much as to off-balance you. Too much emphasis is placed upon the exact percentage of weight on each leg. Ip Ching said that your balance should be carried on your back leg in this case. The point isn't the percentage but the body feel as you move.

Shift back to the right. You'll notice that I'm balanced. More of my weight has shifted to the back (left) leg due to the necessity of the action. Don't mistake this as a tactical fighting lesson. This is about structural mechanics, not fighting application.

Use your elbow power to drop into the what's sometimes called the Chum-Kiu tan-sao position. As we said previously, the palms forward position is stronger than the palms up, so this provides a good basis for understanding a logical defensive guard position.

With good form - that is, with economy of motion - loosely snap your hands into the palm-up position.

Bring the left pak-sao to the right bicep as you push your right palm forward.

Ip Ching performed this movement with lots of snap. His pak-sao sounded like a gun shot when it hit his bicep. You don't need to do it that hard, but you get the idea of the type of snappy power you're developing.

Once more to the right.

Like on the other side, drive the left palm toward the right shoulder line. Be careful to remain balanced.

A thing to note here is how Wing Chun is teaching you to hit with your power line while simultaneously protecting your balance. Putting too much torque into a strike leaves us off balance, easier to counter, and much easier to grab. Much grappling defense is needed by those who throw themselves off balance with bad technique.

Back to the left strike again. Remind yourself to keep your shoulders loose, allowing them to join the thrust of the strike without pulling you off balance. A key point to learn here is that loss of balance and putting weight into a blow aren't synonymous.

Turn to the left, careful to combine the elbow with the lower body.
Finish in the lan-sao position.

Shifting bong-sao/wu-sao #1 from the left side.

*Connect the elbow and hip in your mind again and shift back to lan-
sao. The elbow should be ever so slightly below the wrist line at
completion due to the shifting power line (elbow, hip and shoulder).*

*Bong-wu #2. Be careful not to over shift. Note how you can't see my
amazingly sexy triceps. If you can see the back of your arm, you've
shifting too far. This shows us that this motion is more about
mechanics than application since the bong-sao is a deflection. We
aren't focusing on that here, though. The big idea is the unit
cohesion.*

One more time to the lan-sao position. Watch and make sure you aren't getting sloppy with your footwork. It's easy to let your feet get out of alignment by focusing only on the upper body. In fact, that's a critical error that Chum Kiu seeks to fix.

Third time is a charm.

Lan-sao one last time as we prepare to launch the punch and lop-sao.

Carefully line up your fist. Pulling and hitting, when developed properly, is a deadly skill. The thing is, we must not overdo it or we'll miss and throw ourselves off balance while also pulling the enemy into us. Again...often times grappling commences due to bad offense on the attacker's part. Stay in control of yourself and you can avoid lots of problems in life.

Punch and pull. Dempsey talks about the four ways of hitting power - springing forward, falling forward, upward surge and shoulder whirl. We've just had upward surge and shoulder whirl. We'll get to stepping power in a second. This gives us another. Two-way energy. Pulling them into a blow is nasty business. Of course, he was talking only about boxing so this isn't a criticism of his excellent work. It's to remind us of how important this little aspect is. I can turn you into a devastating hitter.

It can be hard to keep your balance here but shift and use the right fak-sao.

Draw the elbow back to the center. Make sure your hips are still "under you" - that is, pushed forward slightly and you're holding the energy in your stance.

Place your left hand on your right, just below the inner elbow.

Strong two-way energy should be applied from the elbows while staying relaxed.

Huen-sao to grabbing hand.

Right back where we started. This isn't just a thing we do. It isn't arbitrary. It's here to remind us of the critical necessity of integration. Adding or subtracting things that obliterate integration is dangerous business.

NOW WE MOVE on to the **Cho-Ma** or footwork section of Chum Kiu. We remind the reader that all of these actions are "types" and structural principles, not necessarily direct applications. The basics of our footwork is expressed in this section but it's not a ball-and-chain. We move carefully here to develop the correct form. In fighting we move as fast as we can in order to dominate position, to avoid being a target and to access one. If you try and move like this in fighting, forgetting that this is a form, you'll utterly destroy your self-defense ability. That Wing Chun isn't known for great footwork is because people miss this important point and end up moving like some kind of Wing Chun zombie...thinking it's illegal to move fast and low to the floor.

Raise your arm and pause. Make a mental connection, as usual, between the elbow and hip. Stay relaxed.

Turn quickly, using good form, to the left, careful to maintain the elbow-hip connection. Some Wing Chun lineages use this as a push off, as if pushing an enemy away from them as they turn. Others use the elbow as a quick strike as they turn. Both approaches have merit. We suggest you focus not only on those things but on the more important body-feel/mechanic of the 90 degree turn.

The basic kick is now used. The knee should come up and the kick should thrust forward smoothly. The bottom of the foot is used in the basic straight kick.

The "landing" brings you into the bong-wu position. Obviously, this isn't a lesson in tactics. It's a lesson in structural mechanics. Don't fall forward after a kick. Stay balanced! By using the rear-side bong-sao after the basic left leg kick we learn to move as a unit. Going all-in with a single strike is a dangerous gambit. It's like gambling instead of investing. It's like paying your rent with your credit card. You can do it...but it's an accident waiting to happen.

Dropping your hands like this loads the next movement. We're getting ready to learn the proper mechanics of footwork.

To move left, step about a foot with your left and then slide your right the same distance after it. As you do this, bring up your right bong-sao, with the wu-sao behind it. This basically forms a "neutral" position to remind us to bring the body along as a unit. Like with the shifting, loss of unit cohesiveness is a thing to avoid.

Without stepping, drop your hands again.

Again step to your left one foot length. The basic step in Wing Chun is the foot closest to the direction you're going then followed by the "driving foot." This avoids raising one's center of gravity in the midst of combat. Alas, our steps should be small so as to avoid large motions that can off-balance us.

Shift to 90 degrees and drop your elbow as you go. This will give you power for a short punch. The structural principle in play is that when your elbow is below your fist you gain power line support by turning the fist into the palm up position.

Keeping the elbow and hip connection, shift back to the middle - don't just mindlessly turn back to center-facing. This is a power developing movement not to be overlooked. The arm doesn't have much power when moving away from the center, so shifting will give you a needed assist.

Repeat the two-way energy action.

Because I'm off a little to the side of the camera it looks like my arm isn't on center. It is. We wanted to give you, as best we can with still photos, the sense of how far I moved. The Wing Chun footwork is small. Three steps shouldn't carry you more than three feet. It's better to use three or four rapid steps than one long one due to the danger of combat footing. Balance is the currency of fighting. Nothing gets paid without it.

Huen-sao and grab.

Back to scratch and ready to go the other way.

Now we're going to the right.

Raise your knee without telegraphing or loading up.

*You can use the basic kick as high as you want but we suggest
keeping it from the waist down for the best results.*

Come down into a balanced bong-wu position

Low hand position. Ready to step again. The back foot is ready to go as the front foot lifts to initiate the step.

Step and use the bong-wu.

Back to the low hand position. Another point to learn is that attacks in the real world often happen before we're in a fighting position. This is a critical piece of the self-defense puzzle that sporting systems neglect. Our first reaction to a sudden attack may very often require footwork to get off the line. Again, self-defense is the art and science of keeping yourself as safe as possible in the event of an UNPLANNED and UNAVOIDABLE attack. This sequence will naturally look highly eccentric to those who are thinking from sporting presuppositions.

Back to the bong-wu with the step.

With a coordinated shift, drive your punch "into the body of the enemy." The fist, as Dempsey said, gets all the glory but it's only along for the ride. This action is a nifty blow to the body from close range and should be used more often. Kill the body and the fight is over. This should dispel the myth that Wing Chun doesn't have heavy body punches.

As you prepare to shift back to the forward facing position make sure you don't get structurally disorganized. It's very important to develop good habits here since this is what's training your muscle-memory. Make sure you don't bounce in order to gain momentum for the upcoming turn as that's evidence that you're off balance. Focus on using the shift slowly.

Shift back to center being careful to bring your elbow with the shifting hip. Remember that we're getting a "package deal" with the Wing Chun forms. This is a useful technique, yes, but you're always training for good mechanics that can be adjusted to any situation. In other words, no single action of the form is limited to only that expression.

Bring the right hand to the left. Don't get lazy and focus on the hands here. We're working on two-way energy which is derived in this case from the elbows.

The right hand, thrusting forward from the elbow, finishes while the left hand is pulled back - also elbow powered - to the chambered (sout kuen) position.

Use huen-sao, grab and then pull your hand back to the sout-kuen position. This is, again, powered by the elbow and is both a lop-sao and a backward elbow strike action.

Okay now, back to scratch.

Now we shift to the left again but without the elbow turning like the last time. This is the beginning of the LOW BONG SECTION.

The basic kick is used again. A quick note to the reader is that once you get this down you may use variations of the kick. For example, I'm aiming this one more as an upward kick to the groin. There's nothing illegal in using logical variations once you have the basics. The refusal to do so turns Wing Chun into a museum piece rather than a self-defense system. We should be pulling the meat off the bones, so to speak, in order to best understand the structural fundamentals we're learning.

As your left foot comes down, with control of your balance, of course, bring your hands forward in the low bong-sao position. Step simultaneously into the motion so that you go forward into your landing.

The low bong-sao position. Why do we do this? First, it's another reminder that we might be attacked when our hands are down. If an opponent is making a thrust at our stomach, we don't have time to bring our hands up and then down again to block. This is the most direct route to defend the midsection.

Drop your hands back to your side again and prepare for your next movement.

Step forward again while using the double low bong-sao. Another reason this is an important technique to learn is that in modern self-defense if you see a low-line attack it might be a knife thrust. In full application we'd do only one bong-sao rather than two and we'd shift to assist the deflection.

Drop the hands back to your side again. You'll notice that I'm not leaning backward as if I'm advancing into a Category 5 hurricane. My weight is relatively even although the "spring" is carried on the rear leg. Overdoing the lean as some lineages do, placing exorbitant weight on the rear leg, is a dangerous gambit to use in this day and age where there's a grappler under every rock. Stay low to the floor and balanced at all times. Avoid wild extremes.

Step forward again with the double low bong-sao (dai bong).

*Drop the elbows as you step forward with your right leg and lower
your weight. This gives you a heavy jut-sao (dragging) action that
pulls the enemy toward the floor. It teaches us how to use sinking
power with the entire unit rather than just the arms. This concept is
seen again in Section 1 and 3 on the Wooden Dummy. In Section 1
there's a slight shift added to the lop-sao and pull. This teaches us to
remain balanced while destroying that of the enemy. It also shows
us how not to pull the enemy into us, but toward the floor and that's
a critical difference.*

From the crouch, drive up with a double palm strike/push. Wing Chun pushes have a snappy explosiveness built into them. A good push, executed with timing and structure, can end matters due to the fact that it can throw the enemy into, over, and off of things. A Wing Chun fighter should always be eager to help an off-balanced opponent by throwing them via the explosive push. This action here shows the full body getting in on the fun.

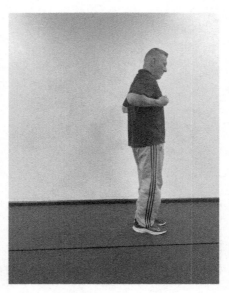

*After turning your hands to tan-sao, then using double huen-sao
and lop-sao, return to the chambered fist position.*

Step your right leg behind the left as seen here. This forms the basic structure of any turning or "spinning" technique. If you were to turn with a hammer-fist or fak-sao, for example, this would be a "spinning strike". You can use whatever technique you'd need with the turn - maybe even an elbow. So much for Wing Chun not having spinning techniques. Those who think that Wing Chun is limited to mere chain punches aren't paying attention to the logical implications of the forms.

Complete the turn. You should be well balanced when you complete the movement.

Basic kick is executed. Obviously the weight is held totally on the left leg. You're advised to practice this at varying speeds - even slowly - so as to develop good body feel and strength in the support leg. As we keep hammering home: balance is key. We have a tendency - a very human one - to play to extremes. We play balance over against agility and movement and vice versa. This section of the form is telling us that we should be able to turn and hit from any angle without loss of balance. What good is balance if we can't do anything with it? And what good is agility if we have no power?

For this photo we slowed things down to show the kick returning to the floor. Though we're going to move forward on the next movement, it's important to note that we don't have to. We could, if necessary, put the kicking leg down and then just as easily step backward. Or sideways.

Step forward with the combined footwork and double low bong-sao.

Relax your hands to the low position.

Step forward again with the double low bong-sao. Incidentally, this action also gives us the idea of the shoulder roll (made most famous methinks by Floyd Mayweather and his renowned Philly-shell. Yes, the Wing Chun fighter can do that too! The mechanics for it are right here.

JASON KOROL

Drop the hands to the low position.

Step forward for the third time with the combined footwork and double low bong-sao.

Step with the back foot as you drop your weight and elbows simultaneously.

Drive upward and FORWARD with the double palm attack. Be careful not to drive the palms upward at an angle lest they lose their structural power. Think of the bench press. If the arms keep going upward rather than forward you'll expose your undercarriage and lose considerable oomph from the attack.

After the palms, use double tan-sao, double huen-sao, and then double lop-sao and return to the chambered fist position.

Pivot slightly toward the left by turning your toes. As you do this, start looking left as though you're addressing a threat across the left shoulder line.

Execute a sweeping/crescent kick. Some lineages use a side kick, which is fine. Because we use the latter during the Wooden Dummy form (Section 2) and the crescent kick isn't practiced elsewhere, we use it here. Though it isn't as useful as the basic straight kick in Wing Chun, it does go to show us that the forms are providing for us a structural education with tactical corollaries. In this case we learn that the most direct kick to a target at this angle is the sweeping kick. In all, use what you need (with non-contradictory mechanics). Wing Chun isn't telling us that we must meet every attack with a vertical punch! Straight hits are more advantageous than round ones but they aren't a straight-jacket.

As you place your foot down, as always, balance is the key thing.

As soon as your foot touches down shift to the left leg and execute a low gum-sao (pressing/pinning hand).

Here's the extension of the low gum-sao action. Notice the balance is shifted to the left leg and the right hand is in wu-sao.

Shift to the right and execute a right low gum-sao and high left tan-sao. You'll notice that it's the right hand - the pressing one - that's got more power in this action. Since the left hand is spreading away it doesn't carry as much power as the pressing hand. You may eschew the tan-sao with the left and instead use a left wu-sao if you want. Our family plays it either way but this one plants the seed idea for the kwan-sao action (rotating hand) in the Dummy form.

Shift again to the left and execute another low gum-sao.

Bring the left hand up to a punch while shifting back to center. This plants the seed for using the extended hand as a weapon rather than retracting it and using the other one. It's an invaluable tool for recovering a lost line expeditiously.

Shift with a long straight right punch. The basic Wing Chun punch can be used long or short depending upon the timing, distance and need. In this case, due to the shift of the power line the straight punch will have increased range and power.

Shift and throw another powerful straight punch with the left. I've seen many families totally ignore this longer straight punch. They do so at their own loss - wrongly concluding that Wing Chun only throws the short straight punch. This conclusion is either steeped in the the fallacy of traditionalism or the either-or fallacy. For example, no one doubts that a pak-sao and punch are Wing Chun yet such an action is never directly seen in the forms. The long straight punch on the other hand is eschewed because they arbitrarily think it's forbidden. But here it is. And even in families that don't play the form this way, it's implied - just like the pak-sao and hit.

Shift again and pow! Learning how to hit with our whole body is a key component to Wing Chun. Take your time with this section and see how it changes your view of the basic straight punch.

Shift back to center and perform the short straight punch.

Here's the famous Wing Chun straight blast. The shoulders and body stay out of this one .

Almost done. I'm going to slide my left foot to my right as I loosely press my hands down and draw a long breath. Do this deliberately because being able to relax under pressure is a massive skill in life that helps in more ways than just in fighting. It certainly helps at the office when the boss yells at you or gives you an impossible deadline and you want to scream at him. Or at your mother-in-law's when she says something passive-aggressive. Or...you get the idea. Relax and breath. Stress is a killer. What good does it do for us to protect ourselves from an enemy but kill ourselves with stress. Relax.

All done. Congratulations. Our advice is to learn the form sequentially - in other words, memorize it first. After this, start zeroing in on specifics and getting it right. There's no such thing as perfection with it. There's always something to improve. One of the major benefits is that it gives us wisdom. It shows us truths we had no way of knowing beforehand. This is important because experience is a painful teacher - giving us the test first and the lesson later. Learning through experience has its place but violence isn't necessarily one of them because we might be dead or gravely injured after the lesson. Our motto shouldn't be "live and learn" but "learn and live."

3

CHUM KIU: WING CHUN'S FIGHTING FORM

O ver-complication. That's the problem. By not keeping the main thing the main thing, we end up focusing valuable - and irreplaceable - training time on minor aspects. This mistake is, alas, because we make a mystery out of something that ought to be really, really, simple. It's a pattern of life, unfortunately... and we're all guilty of it.

Hit the guy.

Move.

Hit and move.

Take his balance and control his hands at close range - either through angle/position and/or contact control. And hit him.

How do we know if our bong-sao is good? Easy. Does it help us do the aforementioned things? If so, the bong is fine. It can always be better, yes, but the goal isn't the perfect bong-sao. The goal is to defend yourself. You aren't fighting to defend Wing Chun. If someone is trying to kill you, you aren't in a struggle to defend the historical integrity of Ip Man or your Sifu. You need to neutralize the threat in order to kiss your wife and children goodnight ever again. Wing Chun, nor anything else under the sun, is an end in and of itself. Your bong-sao is effective only insofar as it assists the primary goal of self-defense, which is to keep you as safe as possible in the event of unavoidable violence. Perfect Wing Chun is like perfect hand-gunnery...it's not the point. Using the tool for personal defense is the point. And personal defense is needed in the worst possible scenario.

Wing Chun is, therefore, a personal warfare system to be deployed in that sort of calamitous event. It either meets the goals of non-contradictory self-defense or it doesn't, right? The errors we see so often are either saying "just do whatever works" (hard pragmatism) or "your Wing Chun must look like this..." (hyper-traditionalism). We're advocating for neither. What we're saying is that literally everything in the Wing Chun system is designed to help us achieve success in personal combat. Wing Chun is designed to achieve the goal of the utmost safety in a no-holds barred confrontation where terrain, immediate environment, targets such as eyes and windpipes, weapons, and opponent or opponents are all accounted for. That's a tall order.

Hence the forms.

Yes, Wing Chun is a personal warfare system. It's like any other tool of self-defense. It's like a Glock or a Mossberg 12-guage. The major difference, of course, is that firearms are already made. You have to "make yourself", so to speak. As the incredibly handsome and often plagiarized Sifu Tony Massengill says, "in Wing Chun, you're making yourself the weapon." In the first form, Siu Lim Tao, you were building that weapon - learning how your body worked and providing the foundation needed so as to avoid the common errors of fighting. Sifu David Peterson, he of the Wong Shun Leung school, likened SLT to going to the range to fire your handgun. In so doing you're shooting at a stationary target from a stable position. Chum Kiu, the good Mr. Peterson says, is like shooting at a moving target from a mobile position.

Absolutely.

We add to that (not as though those esteemed Wing Chun masters need my input but, hey, this is my book, right?) the fact that any firearms instructor will obsess about safety. If they don't, they're a hack because the first rule is that we shoot to live, not kill, and mishandling a firearm and accidentally shooting yourself or someone else is literally the worst thing you can do with a gun. Anyone who doesn't think so is exactly the type of fellow you don't want to go shooting with. Competent firearm folks obsess about safety because they keep the main thing the main thing. Thus, the Big Four are always on their mind.

Assume it's loaded.

Keep it pointed in a safe direction.

Keep your booger hook off the bang switch.

Know what's beyond your target.

All "accidents" with firearms are violations of these rules, which is why we refer to them as the Big Four. Take care and abide by these rules and you've ruled out the worst thing that can happen. It's such an enormous responsibility (having a firearm in your hands) that any flippant handling or careless attitude morally disqualifies one from being a self-defender. In other words, there's no such thing as an "accidental" discharge. It's negligence.

Why do we hammer this point? Glad you asked.

Siu Lim Tao is your gun safety rules for hand-to-hand. It identifies, whether we're aware of it or not, the common mistakes we make in fighting and trains us to avoid them at a neuromuscular level. In other words, it trains our "Spidey-senses" to alert us when we're about to commit a technical blunder. I cover all this in the Siu Lim Tao book in case you haven't already got it (not necessarily a shameless plug because the author assumes you're familiar with Wing Chun's first form while reading a book on the second one...not that an extra book sale would hurt...go ahead, buy one...buy one hundred and give them to friends...all those sales will make my wife happy).

Well, Chum Kiu brings us to actual application. Just knowing how not to shoot yourself or your mother-in-law by mistake does not a gunfighter make. That requires how to draw the weapon, moving with it, reloads and all that fun stuff. Well, this is where lots of us mess up. We think, okay, I've learned the primary structures of the first form. Good for me. I know about the centerline and all that. I'm good to go.

Not so fast.

The second form isn't like the first. The hint is in the name. What are we seeking in the "bridge seeking form?" A bridge implies an enemy. Now we're hunting. A bridge seeker, insofar as the personal art of war is concerned, is a person who's seeking to dominate an otherwise unavoidable enemy through the combination of superior position and technical skill. Again: in the moral universe we're talking about, self-defense is something that's forced upon us. This isn't a match or some kind of ego fight. Sure, some people do things or say things that are highly objectionable. Sure, they deserve to get punched in the face. But in the words of William Munny in Clint Eastwood's Unforgiven, "We've all got it coming to us, kid."

None of us are sinless. That's not the point. The point is that we're forced to defend ourselves because retreat or avoidance is impossible. This is the only context in which self-defense is allowed and that's the moral foundation we're assuming here. That said, the best defense is a "good" offense. A good offense isn't a reckless charge but a coordinated assault combining tactical precision and technical execution in a non-contradictory manner. A good offense is Chum Kiu. It's a package-deal. Chum Kiu takes the lessons of SLT and applies them. CK makes us a hunter. A bridge seeker is an advantage seeker. Mindless aggression and cowardice are flip sides of the same coin of incompetence; they're evidence of lack of emotional control.

So, if the combat is unavoidable Wing Chun teaches us how to attack the attack. It teaches us good offense through the integration of tactical/technical elements. It does this without leaving out relevant detail. Boxing is a great self-defense method due to its brutal simplicity. Heavy firepower that's mobile! That's awesome. The problem is that boxing does leave out critical detail. Bruce Lee called it "over daring". What about groin kicks and all that? It's not that no boxer can adjust to foul tactics but that's the point...adjustments absolutely need to be made. Wing Chun is very much like boxing (much more than many believe) with one huge caveat: it doesn't leave out the foul tactics but assumes them. Dirty fighting is baked into the cake. It must be because all-out personal warfare (self-defense) is by its very nature dirty business.

Pushing. Pulling. Locking. Breaking. Throwing. Tripping. Gouging. Kicking. Punching. All of it is in here.

Welcome to Chum Kiu, Wing Chun's personal art of war.

4

THE BIGGEST PROBLEM IN WING CHUN

I'll just come right out and say it. There's no sense in beating around the bush - not that we can because most fighters have footwork so bad, they'll likely trip and fall into the bush. But, seriously, that's the thing: bad footwork. Nor can we dance around the subject. That requires footwork too. Nope, nope. We can't skip out either. That's footwork too, right? We can't avoid it at all. Evasion takes footwork too.

Okay. I'll stop now (at least for a little while anyway).

The primary thing that's going to make a self-defense system effective or not is how well it moves. And not just moves, as in any old way, or else dancers and gymnasts are self-defenders, but how well it maneuvers the ready position. It's a package deal. You see, the issue with footwork is the iceberg problem. When we see combat, we quite often only notice the striking or the technique that scores. Lost to us is the distance and timing that went into the technique. That's the stuff under the surface. Looking at technique only, insofar as self-defense goes, is like getting married based only on the looks of a woman. Character counts. It's the same with fighting. It's the stuff under the surface that makes all the difference.

In Wing Chun this is particularly prominent. Because the hand techniques are so dominant, other aspects - especially footwork - receive little attention and fanfare. And you might say that due to the unique personality and coolness of things like chi-sao, that Wing Chun practitioners wholly overlook good footwork. The hand-based drills are important, indeed. They're deadly and efficient. They're unique in the pantheon of martial arts. But without the footwork to get us into position, they're useless. It's like we're a bunch of dudes obsessing about the awesome engine but forget to notice that there's no air in the tires. Or there are no tires at all.

Let's put it another way. A military that has air/naval superiority over their enemy can choose, for the most part, when and where a battle is going to take place. The ability to move troops efficiently is essential to warfare. In the Vietnam War, the Vietcong and North Vietnamese Army (NVA) were thoroughly outmatched by America's overwhelming air and naval power. The NVA barely had a life vest much less a navy. Likewise, their Air Force was non-existent. They neutralized these significant American advantages by using the jungle for cover. They built bridges a foot or so under water so as to be invisible from the air and, therefore, immune to bombing during troop movement. It was this way that they ferried about, undetected by the technologically advanced enemy. (America responded by using Agent Orange to kill the foliage. Of course, that also led to a host of birth defects and cancers and all that...but we had a war to win...nothing to see here...carry on).

Nevertheless, these were adjustments only. Unable to move as quickly and efficiently as the U.S., they took an absolute pounding. They paid the price in blood. In many ways America doesn't have the greatest military on the planet as is commonly assumed. It has the best ability to project power. Absent our air and naval power, forced to fight it out on the ground, it remains to be seen how well we'd fare against another significant land force. Or, if someone figures out a way to neutralize our (America's) naval and air supremacy, perhaps with some new technology, our vacation from history would be instantly over. We'd be like Ivan Drago when Rocky cut him. *"Whoa! He can bleed."*

We can see the horrors of trench warfare, the great carnage...the mind-numbing slaughter, and rightly recoil. The battlefield casualties were horrifying. Facing machine gun nests and heavy shelling, the plan for attack was to "go over the top". That's what they called it. The heart of propaganda is the heart of the salesman. They're the same thing except that the salesman works at a company or store and doesn't have the coercive weight of government behind them. To go over the top has a courageous ring to it, does it not? It smacks of heroism and bravery. It sounds a whole lot better than "get out there and run faster than they can shoot."

That was basically the plan. Run at their entrenchments before their machine guns make Swiss cheese out of you. Yep. Run fast. Through shell craters and barbed wire. Faster than bullets one supposes. The European powers, in the years before 1914, had been beating up on technologically disadvantaged colonies in Africa and Asia. It was like an up-and-coming boxer wiping out tomato cans, making mincemeat out of no-hopers, scoring quick KO's.

But when they fought each other - each side equally armed - they found out that no one had any defense. They'd never fought anyone with the technology to punch back. They were like that undefeated fighter finally running into someone who could counter them. Carnage ensued. It was the same in the U.S. Civil War. The casualties and death boggle the mind because soldiers were forced to run at enemy positions. The basic plan was to advance faster than the enemy could shoot...or to do so with more soldiers than could be shot as they advanced on a fixed position.

"Go ahead, kid...run over there and kill them!" The officers said.

"Ah...sir...it's like several hundred yards. Won't they shoot me before I get there?"

"Run fast, kid."

And that's all we need to know about warfare between the time of repeating rifles and tanks and air power.

The lesson in every field of combat, from military to hand-to-hand, is that he who rules the movement has a significant advantage. He who can optimally position his firepower before their enemy can is going to enjoy greater success. The side that must react to that positional advantage, if they're going to prevail, must do so while absorbing a beating. The Soviet Union beat Nazi Germany with the Randall "Tex" Cobb strategy of fighting. The problem for this is that we know who Tex Cobb was because he had a singular ability to take punches. His chin was legendary. It wasn't a good fighting strategy and not one we should emulate.

Another example was the Comanche. We often think about the Indian Wars and see in our minds the image of fierce warriors on horseback out on the open plains. The thing is, until settlers encountered the Comanche, they'd never seen Indians on horseback. None of the Eastern tribes fought that way. They were all grounded, so to speak. The Comanche, and no one knows exactly how, for that's lost to history, were master horsemen.

Somewhere along the line the Comanche, a backward and nomadic tribe of no particular military might, happened upon the multitude of horses left by the Spanish. Who taught them to break, breed and ride the Mustangs is anyone's guess. What we do know for certain is that unlike anyone else, the Comanche could fight on horseback. Their children could ride at full gallop and reach down to pick up things on the ground. I can barely teach 7 year-olds to raise their hand before speaking and their kids were already riding full speed and firing arrows.

No one else was able to fight on horseback quite like the Comanche. Their grown warriors were deadly at 30 yards with the arrow and could fire more than a dozen in the time it took settlers to shoot their guns once! And, yes, they'd do this at full speed. They were a terrifying enemy to face and in short order they dominated what is now whole states. They almost exterminated the Apache. Again, as always, the key to their dominance was their mobility. Mobility took them from being an obscure and weak tribe to arguably the greatest fighting force North America had ever seen by the time the War for Independence was going on across the continent.

The point is that without footwork we have two choices. First, we must overwhelm the enemy before he can fire back. That's basically the whole plan. It's a drastic gambit. If that doesn't work, we're left with option number two, which is having the ability to walk through his return fire. So, in a nutshell, absent footwork, our plan is to blast through the enemy's front door and dare him to stop us.

Now some might argue that their tan-sau or some other defensive coverage is all they need. Yes, that might work.

In a movie.

In a demonstration.

But in a serious scrap where the other fella isn't cooperating and he's throwing heat at us, full speed and like we slept with his wife, kicked his dog, and slapped his momma, that doesn't work. The folks that jabber on about having done this are either lying or were markedly stronger than their enemy. Sure, I can drive my Tundra over a Corolla. But that's not the point at hand. What will I do if I'm the smaller party? What if the other guy hits hard? You know...what happens if it's like World War One and not a one-sided butt kicking?

The good news is that Wing Chun isn't as stupid and senseless as many of its practitioners. It's a system of scientific movement. And what we find in Chum Kiu is pure and unadulterated genius. The issue is that it's all so subtle that we miss it. And we miss it exactly because it's subtle. This is a videogame and porn consuming culture, after all, so we're hardwired to look for truth in grand and bombastic ways. Subtlety often eludes us. The Wing Chun footwork is exactly that: subtle, quick, low to the floor, shifting and stepping in the most economical manner possible. And we do this while also punching, kicking, pushing, and/or pulling. That's the goal.

5

THE FOUNDATION: YJKYM

When we start talking about footwork we're talking about foundation. I mean, what is it that we're moving, right? As simple as this seems, it's a critical point that's missed because we get sloppy in our thinking. We don't stop and ask exactly what something means. This is particularly true in things that everyone thinks they know. Money. Love. Right and wrong. And yes, footwork.

People wrongly assume that the mere act of moving is footwork. But that's dangerous oversimplification. That's like thinking because a woman is beautiful, she's also nice. It's like thinking anyone can drive (and a simple trip to the store in most cities will quickly disabuse you of that fanciful notion). No. Stevie Wonder certainly can't drive, right? I mean, he can press the gas pedal and use the steering wheel, but then there's the whole problem of crashing into stuff he can't see.

That's like footwork "just because" ...that's like moving for the sake of it.

Footwork in self-defense is, like everything else in existence, a specific thing (the law of identity). To say footwork at all, without carefully defining it, is sloppy thinking. Now, being sloppy when you're making a sandwich means you have a messy kitchen. That won't kill a man...unless you lived with my grandmother. A messy kitchen might have, according to her old-ways ethical code, warranted a cast-iron frying pan to the noggin. But for most of us, that's no big deal. Sloppy thinking about combat, on the other hand, is a whole other issue. It's like making random jokes about bombs at the airport. Or telling your girl how pretty her friend is. Don't do it.

And this is where the Yi Ji Kim Yung Ma comes in. That is, of course, the basic training stance that every Wing Chun fighter learns on the first day. It's the stance you're left in while doing the first form, Siu Lim Tao.

A few things to say about that.

First, anyone who's been around a gym or martial arts school knows that there are differing levels of coordination in students/members. Some people naturally, by the gift of God, have better balance than others. This natural blessing isn't the end of the story, though. Everyone has trouble once they start moving and firing. And everyone has serious trouble when there are punches flying at THEIR face. It requires discipline and skill to maintain one's balance while under fire.

No technique, including the fook-sao pictured here, will work if we don't have the correct foundation.

Second, balance is the critical key for being able to both see incoming attacks and deliver firepower downrange. Once a self-defender is off balance they've lost both their field of vision and their ability to expeditiously deliver pain to the enemy. The loss of timing and accuracy are direct results of loss of balance. And the loss of balance is due to poor footwork.

Third, the primary definition of real fighting is a non-cooperative, violent encounter. An enemy is not going to stand still. Resistance, aggression, and pressure are critical parts of this equation. That being said, footwork is essential in that constant adjustments need to be made due to this resistance. In fact, due to this reality, and all the variables it brings with it (such as environmental hazards, size of the enemy, weapons...like the aforementioned cast iron frying pan, for example) it's logical to say that footwork is the first, second, and third thing to consider.

Fourth, regarding the environmental hazards of all-out combat, the loss of balance is the primary concern for fighting. Falling and hitting your head on a hard surface can be deadly. In fact, just the other day, as I write this, a twenty-something year-old man died in Forrest Hills, New York, an area I'm quite familiar with personally, because he jumped a turnstile to avoid paying the subway fare. He tripped. His head broke his fall. When there's a fight between the human head and concrete, concrete is undefeated.

Curbs. Stairs. Cluttered rooms. Bystanders. Clueless and oblivious writers typing away on their MacBook who don't know enough to get out of harm's way. But seriously, I like to bring people outside at my martial arts school. In the back we have a nice grassy area. It looks flat until you start moving and then you realize it gently slopes and has a few small holes that are, if walking, no big deal, but if moving quickly, might cause a serious injury.

And this, my friends, is precisely why we practice the YJKYM for so long. It provides the "body feel" or muscle-memory we need. If gives us the foundation and it's this - that foundation - that we're moving. It's the standard we keep appealing back to so as to not make a shipwreck of our self-defense system. So, when we say "good footwork" we mean the expeditious movement of our firepower and that firepower is coming from the YJKYM. Quick and rapid stepping, and shifting too, that carries the YJKYM to more advantageous positions is the goal. Thus, we don't fight directly in our YJKYM...we fight from it.

So, yes, absolutely...practice your YJKYM. Practice, practice, practice. But you've got to start moving that base which the first form developed. Don't stop there. That's like seeing the girl, meeting the girl, wooing her, marrying her and then...being content to hold hands on your honeymoon. No one is ever going to win a fight standing in the YJKYM. The idea is to use that base as a principled guide to one's footwork and striking and other elements (like pushing/pulling). Because of the speed and uncertainty of combat we must have highly trained fundamentals designed to give us principled adaptability. This is the YJKYM in a nutshell. It's the foundation of Wing Chun.

6

TAXONOMY OF FIGHTING
FOOTWORK

Taxonomy of Fighting Footwork
Bad or fuzzy definitions kill. Well, insofar as combat is concerned anyway. We aren't suggesting that adding a little too much pepper to your dinner will kill you. Of course, telling your girl that she's starting to look a little chubby in those jeans might do the trick. That's a flawed definition right there. In actuality, though, when it comes to certain things - and fighting is definitely one of them - the necessity of sound definitions is paramount.

The issue in front of us goes back to the biggest problem in Wing Chun and self-defense. We do a poor job of classifying everything. We say vague things like "in a fight" without having bothered to define what we mean by that. This creates a vacuum and it's often filled by half-truths (like sport fighting) or outright contradictions. Let's not do that.

A fight, as far as we're concerned, is an *unavoidable* altercation where our life, liberty, and safety are on the line. If one's basic rights to life aren't at stake a "fight" simply can't be a self-defense situation. It may be a good many other things, yes, but pure self-defense it's not. In the first Ip Man movie (the really good one before they started going comic-book level absurdity on us) the venerable master was forced to fight the occupying Japanese Leader, a general with a love of martial art skill, or else he'd be executed. That's not an exception to the rule, incidentally, since Ip Man's life (in the movie, that is) was threatened and the conflict was unavoidable. It's an indirect realization of the definition of self-defense.

Since the clash is unavoidable, we must logically assume that footing and environment will play key roles. A match in a ring or a cage, for instance, besides being prearranged, has the critical element of secure footing and, just as exigent, safe borders. A border is the area around the combat zone. Ropes or a cage keep the combatants from injury. The borders of self-defense might very well be exceedingly dangerous. It could be a flight of stairs, a cliff, a curb leading into moving traffic, and so on. Even things like drywall, cabinets, countertops, chairs, and tables can be exceedingly dangerous. Whacking your melon into a shelf is about as much fun as going clothes shopping with your girl (although, if you're in the store long enough, the aforementioned might seem like a reasonable idea).

Another aspect of self-defense to consider isn't just footing (mats, pavement, grass, hiking trail, stairwell, etc.) but obstacles. There may be other people (perhaps your family and kids) in the way. Look around you and see all the tripping hazards. Real fights occur in places where people are at, right? A good many martial systems disregard this to their peril, which, incidentally, invalidates them as a true science of self-defense. Again, we aren't talking about putting too much pepper on your eggs. This is life-or-death. The blatant disregard of the footwork-environment-border issue in most training today is evidence of our loss of martial focus. Most of us in the west, fat and happy and sipping lattes, simply can't imagine being in a life-or-death struggle in a confined space. Some can't imagine combat at all. Some prefer not to think those "dark" thoughts. Others, usually young and competitive, think a ring or cage is the pinnacle of combat and ignore the limits of ritualized combat.

Unavoidable fights also might include more than one opponent. This alone mitigates against ground fighting for self-defense since that eliminates one's footwork. Ground fighting is, as we've seen in

MMA over the years, very effective if the environmental factors are strictly controlled. An angry girlfriend or opportunistic friend of your enemy, if you're in a vulnerable position, might take the opportunity to find out how hard they can kick. It's logical for us to not offer our head for their experiment.

Unavoidable fights might also include weapons or foul tactics. Expecting the enemy in self-defense situations to play fair is like expecting congressmen to tell the whole truth. Or like expecting the Cowboys not to choke in the playoffs. Or expecting traffic to zoom along when you're in a hurry. Or me not to use bad jokes. In any event, if the enemy wants to bite, gouge, or stab, we must do what we can to improve our odds. Ground fighting as a primary discipline is antithetical to safety in that event. This is to say that no methodology could be worse than ground fighting when dealing with multiple opponents, foul tactics, and weapons.

To that end, we know that our footwork must be both stable and mobile. It can't be one or the other. It must be capable of both. Moreover, the mobility must not compromise the stability of one's ready-position, nor the other way around. Fighting footwork, for the reasons just detailed, must be, without contradiction, stable and mobile.

Second, it must be ambidextrous. In Wing Chun we preach "a leg forward but not a side forward." Blading-off is great for sparring environments where the targets, footing, and borders are controlled. But the square-on ready-position is preferred, albeit with one leg slightly forward, since that provides no advance target (like the leading leg too far out front for takedowns and kicks), multi-lateral stability, and quick access to moving in any direction. The demands of self-defense fighting require that we're able to move not just on any surface but in any direction. This requires that we're able to use either leg as our forward leg and either leg as our "driving" leg. For this reason, Wing Chun fighting footwork is all-wheel drive.

Oftentimes in Wing Chun I've heard teachers preach about the advantages of a squared-on stance, but rarely have I heard better footwork options detailed. The focus is completely upon the access to both hands and feet as offensive tools. This is true, yes, but those tools are useless if we're off balance or unable to cover ground quickly. Good footwork must be able to navigate the aforementioned realities of self-defense fighting without compromise. Other systems, boxing in particular, are said by many to have superior footwork to Wing Chun. But that's only because they have left this relevant discussion out of their evaluations.

One last element of footwork to consider before we move on: timing. We'll deal with this subject in greater detail in a follow-up volume on Biu Jee, but suffice it to say that good timing is the "secret power" of great martial artists. The ability to do the right thing at the right time is critical. The thing to note, though, is that timing and position are inextricably linked. In combat there's no such thing as good timing from the wrong spot, nor proper position at the wrong time. They're one unit insofar as application is concerned. To that end, a Wing Chun fighter who's trained to seek superior position for attack and defense will discover that their timing has improved. By "fighting" for superior position over the enemy one discovers that proper application of technique follows. But because most students think primarily about technique first, and position/footwork only as an auxiliary (if at all), their technique suffers.

Good footwork is good timing because it's relational/positional.

Therefore Wing Chun footwork is our best bet for self-defense.

7

WHY WE DISREGARD FOOTWORK

We're too focused on the hands/weaponry and this leads us to think that it's bad Wing Chun to use something other than our hands to solve a problem.

The hands of Wing Chun are super cool. They just are. Nothing is cooler (at least to us) than a quick and flashy eruption of hands from chi-sao, right? It's awesome. But we must be careful. We've got to stay objective.

There's always been the famous line for this...you know, "don't concentrate on the finger or you'll miss all the heavenly glory it's pointing at." That's certainly apropos. The problem is that I don't struggle with that particular ailment. I've never been tempted to stare at someone's finger if they're pointing at something. I've heard of weird dudes with foot fetishes but never someone with a finger fetish. Anyway, I have in the past compromised by objectivity because of a pretty girl. I'm sure something like that has happened to all of us at some point. (I have that effect on women too, I'm sure. Momma always said I was handsome!).

I once fell for this girl who had these amazing Susanna Hoffs-type eyes. If you don't know who Susanna is, put this down and go look her up. If you don't fall instantly and entirely in love, I forbid you from reading any further. She was gorgeous. You're obviously brain damaged if you don't think so. And you're probably evil too. You probably hate puppies and kittens and never wave anyone through when you arrive the same time at a 4-way stop. You can't be trusted and should be banished from polite society.

Wait...what were we talking about?

Oh, yeah. Sorry.

But, seriously, it's a case of infatuation. Infatuation causes a man to lose his perspective, just like the girl with the Susanna eyes that bewitched me body and soul (Mr. Darcy would have been much cooler if he did Wing Chun). The cool hand stuff infatuates us and causes us to overlook other relevant detail...like footwork (and, in my case, that the pretty eyes were attached to a crazy girl...sigh). Yep, the cool hand stuff of chi-sao infatuates us into thinking that that's where we should be spending the vast majority of our training time and at the expense of something "so elemental" as footwork. Never mind that the height of simplicity in fighting is being in the right place at the right time and that is literally the definition of footwork. Never mind that no matter how crazy your crossing hand skills are, no matter how "John Wick" you can get with your training partners, that unless you can move quickly and decisively, you're a sitting duck.

We think it's running

Good footwork isn't running. It's the disciplined transportation of your structure to a place where you're safer than your enemy. It's the ability to out-maneuver your foe, nullifying his attack by angle and distance and making him pay for his lack of positional skill. Running is running. Good fighting footwork is using distance and angles to shut down his attack and facilitate your own.

Ego gets involved here. If a guy was coming after you with a gun and you ducked for cover while drawing your weapon, you wouldn't think that was running, would you? Why do people lose their tactical mindset when it comes to hand-to-hand combat? It's all ego and bluster. The same principles apply in empty hand combat as with guns and knives...and everything else for that matter. I don't want to give my opponent a chance to get started. I don't want a fair fight. The stakes are too high. This isn't a game and I'm not going to gain anything after the fight that I didn't already have before it anyway. If I have something to gain from violence that means that I'm the bad guy. Self-defense means protecting what you already have from a person who's trying to take it (immorally). Using footwork, barriers, and any other means of movement to assist in this goal isn't merely a good idea but essential to one's success.

Self-defenders who don't try and gain every edge they can are confusing the point. Never concede to a set of man-made rules that only helps your enemy. It's a fight for survival and our footwork should be as fast and diversified as our hand actions. Never, never, never forget this. In a fight, make it you and everything at your disposal against the bad guy. Confusing training drills and/or sport combat with real-world violence can be a deadly mistake. It's like a rape victim asking the rapist to light a candle and play some soft music. We aren't talking about a match. This isn't prize fighting because the "prize" is your life...and you already have that.

People think it's running because they've been duped into thinking of sport. Even in movies you see a good guy throw down his weapon in a fight with the bad guy should the latter lose his. Honor or some such thing as that. But that's like having Nazis break down your door and you telling them where you're hiding the Jews because lying is bad. No. That's a categorical fallacy. Self-defense is any means necessary to save your life. It's wrong if I shoot a guy in a boxing match. That's dishonorable (illegal too one supposes). But using angles and footwork to minimize the enemy's ability to get at you is the smartest thing you can do in a self-defense situation. There are no judges to critique you. Survival is the goal and footwork makes you a harder target to hit/hurt. Period. A stationary target is something we should never be.

It's very hard, it only looks easy, so people move on to "other stuff."

Good footwork subsumes other exigent issues of self-defense. Courage. Timing. Vicious patience. Tactical skill in reading the intent of the enemy. Correct judgment of distance and striking accuracy.

Thus, to see a man/woman evade a swing and then counter with a straight punch or kick, is to see an amazing coordination of technical/tactical skill in a hurry. Courage not to freeze or overreact (thereby destroying their balance and ability to instantly counter). Timing to move in sync with the enemy. Vicious patience to wait to throw a telling blow until the opening presented itself, which, indeed, requires a fine-tuned aggression that's controlled by one's discipline. Anger and fear, unchecked, will destroy one's timing and accuracy. Lastly, the correct judgment of distance is also on display...the defender may need a single short step...or maybe two or even three.

There's an old saying about a woman who was walking in Central Park in New York, and she happened to cross paths with a man who offered to do her portrait for $50. She recognized him as a famous artist and was exuberant. "Yes...of course! Oh, to have my likeness drawn by such a famous man! Wow!" So, she sat down and in five scant minutes of work he produced a beautiful rendering of her. She was overjoyed. To see herself as the artist did - so lovely and with several personal touches a lesser artist would have omitted.

But then she said, "Wait...that only took you five minutes."

"Yes...so?"

"Well, $50 is a lot of money for only a few minutes of work."

The artist smiled and said, "25 years and five minutes, my dear."

His point is our point. It took years of training to make it look that easy.

People who work on footwork and timing know how important they are. And they know it only looks easy. It's hard, so very hard. It's the ability to make quick adjustments of angle and/or distance in order to nullify the enemy's offense and simultaneously secure your own. To the untrained eye it doesn't look like you did anything. The lack of wisdom on this point leads many to focus nearly all their training efforts on the accumulation of technical skill absent footwork.

8

WHY FOOTWORK IS YOUR SUPERPOWER

T o have superior mobility in fighting should be the goal of every fighter. The alternatives are illogical. If we can't outmaneuver our foe then we're relegated to having to exchange heavy fire in set-piece battles. With everyone. This demands that we're never pitted against someone who's markedly larger, stronger, or capable of taking insane amounts of damage. If any of that happens then we're relegated to having to "bridge the gap" by absorbing damage.

Having better footwork, however, allows us the blessing of being able to make instant adjustments. If someone's style or reach or quirkiness gives us trouble, it's footwork that can save the day. Again, it's like having a superior Air Force. It makes sending in the ground forces much, much easier.

Allows you to control the position - bad position kills

Chum Kiu's footwork structure is the step-and-slide. It shows the foundation of Wing Chun footwork. It moves only in one direction in the form but it's a "type" that can be used however we need. Using the step-slide principle and structure, one can move efficiently in any direction without compromising their balance. And since the movements are so small, they can be used to gain an edge by virtue of everyone else using either terrible footwork (crossing their feet, etc.) or sport footwork that's designed for safe terrain.

The step-slide footwork of Chum Kiu, when mastered, can be used on any rhythm. Quick step, quick step, pause, thrusting step... the same structure allows you to dominate the timing and position of the altercation by using the super-efficient step-slide to make your enemy travel (to use an old boxing saying). Bad fighters just try and hit people, or grab them, and footwork is an afterthought. Good fighters use footwork to hit people. Good fighters work hard to get "the drop" on the enemy.

Focus on footwork keeps our minds set on tactical control so that the technique follows, as it should. Reversing this order leads to trouble.

Simultaneous Attack & Defense

The more technique you're using (or trying to use) the more you need footwork. Small, rapid steps allow you to do two things at once - and that is position yourself safely while simultaneously hitting/controlling the dude.

Many Wing Chun people are taught poorly on this point. They stand straight in front of the enemy and try to use simultaneous attack and defense with a tan sau and hit - or something like that. This puts them in a reaction zone where they must be perfect in catching the correct angle of a blow thrown by a bad guy they've never fought before. Don't underestimate the importance of this point. You likely won't be defending yourself against someone you've had the chance to study. This is something that's rarely mentioned in class but is of critical importance. You shouldn't be getting into fights with classmates, right? You won't have a "feeling out" phase if someone kicks in your front door.

To correctly parry and hit (block and hit) while directly in front of the enemy requires great precision. Any personal variance of a strike thrown your way can disrupt your timing. In a way of seeing it, with the stakes high, the intensity volume cranked to 10, you must be perfect. The enemy merely needs to be close. Footwork makes your defense easier and faster since you have to cover less angles than if you're standing straight in front of someone. If you remain directly in-line, though, you have multiple angles to account for against an enemy you've never had a chance to study.

Those odds suck.

If a guy throws a haymaker at you and you stay in the danger zone, you have to be perfect in your execution. But if you use footwork and/or shifting (providing you couldn't stop hit him in the first place, of course) you can get out of the way and either hit as you move or counterattack immediately after. Since so many fights start with an ambush style launch, we can logically assume that the enemy often has a slight edge in timing, which makes footwork all the more important. (Many critics of this approach, incidentally, assume they'll be perfectly set-up to receive the attack, but the nature of all-out self-defense contradicts this presumption).

Maximizes adaptability

Confidence should come from your training. With proper discipline you should believe that if you get someone out of position, anyone, that you can take them out of the fight. Arrogance, on the other hand, is thinking that you don't need position and that the same thing can't happen to you. In this way, overconfidence happens not when we think we're really good but when we think others aren't. Good footwork is the hallmark of fighters who respect their enemy and, consequently, work hard at out-positioning him.

There's always a careful balance of respect and fear. We should respect our foe. Fear can paralyze us but respect for him is a healthy sense of realism. It's the respect for how quickly things can go wrong. It's the recognition that we don't know everything and, therefore, this drives us to fight hard to always maintain positional control. Arrogant fighters are those who disregard the enemy's capacity. Realistic self-defenders know that anyone - anyone at all - who gets the drop on us can hurt us.

This mentality works its way out in our footwork and attention to positional detail. Watch how fast the great Wong Shun Leung moved. He was like a Wing Chun Mike Tyson. He closed the gap with lighting footwork that, alas, was deceptive! He would start one direction, notice the adjustment of his foe, and then zip the other way and crash in from the newly exposed line. This is a great example of Wing Chun's blitzkrieg type of attack. It's not straight forward like a zombie - *it's straight forward into the exposed line of the enemy who couldn't match your positional adjustments.* Wong Shun Leung was perhaps Wing Chun's most accomplished fighter exactly because his footwork was as fast as his hands. Slow and/or directionally limited footwork is a surefire way to combative disaster and the late master knew that.

Another area where this is key is in the event of multiple opponents.

The ability to move fast and change both the direction and timing of one's steps is the key to surviving such a clash. And the thing is, everyone knows that they must do this against more than one attacker - yet they don't train for it. If we always train for this reality and we only have one opponent, that's great! But if we hardly ever do, or never, and then we have a second or third foe, we likely won't prevail. A fighter with poor footwork is like a soldier in a firefight with only a few rounds of ammo. He must be deadly accurate or he's dead. Footwork is like having unlimited ammo. It keeps you in the fight until it's over and you're safe.

This brings us to another exigency. We don't have one set of skills for one-on-one, another for multiple opponents, and yet another in case a weapon is involved. This is the deadly fantasy rotting away the foundation of many contemporary fighting arts. Like a house with a hidden termite problem, thinking we can simply adjust our reflexes during the dreadful crisis of violence is a recipe for disaster. Muscle-memory is a fickle thing. When I first moved to the south from New York I was unaware of how much profanity I had in my everyday language. The F-bomb was a bad word but all the other ones were, well, conversation enhancers as far as I knew. Getting myself to stop using salty language was quite a chore. And that's just talk we're talking about, right? Do you really think that your years of training to clinch is going to altered under pressure? Do you really think that years of BJJ will be easily overridden in there's a second opponent?

In our school we're always training for the *totality* of self-defense rather than for the predictability of sport or dojo/school drilling. We always assume there will be an unfair fight against more than one opponent and this is why footwork must be trained scientifically. Under deadly pressure is no time to try and learn new skills and do new things. Under pressure we sink to the level of our discipline; we don't rise to the level of the challenge.

9

UNLOCKING WING CHUN THROUGH SUN TZU'S ART OF WAR

The misapprehension of Sun Tzu's classic work, Art of War, is instructive for Wing Chun students. On the one hand, it represents our current generation's "concrete bound" thinking. That is to say, it exposes our wholesale refusal/inability to think in categories. We think in brute facts. It's not entirely our fault, though. Due to our poor education (it being anti-theoretical) we're very often relegated to thinking about subjects with no context. A brute fact, so that we're clear, is something that we see; a disassociated thing; a thing in a vacuum. A thing with no context.

Wisdom, on the other hand, is the non-contradictory apprehension of the context of a fact/thing. A fool, to use the Biblical idea, isn't someone who's uneducated. It's someone who sees life in brute facts - in hardened compartments rather than interrelated categories all running to a sound foundation.

For example, when people talk about political candidates they rarely stop and take the time to establish what their theory of politics is in the first place. They don't do that because they can't. And they can't because they haven't taken the time to arrive at a non-contradictory definition of government and state. To do so requires a theory of ethics, which needs to stand atop a theory of knowledge (epistemology), which demands a foundation of metaphysics. We all notice that political discourse is in the toilet but it's down there precisely because we haven't taken the time to establish the fundamentals. That's why there's so much rancor in political discussions. It's all about personal attacks because it can't be about fundamentals because we don't understand them. A clogged toilet, like a clogged mind, needs to be cleared or else everything starts to stink.

There's nothing wrong with being wrong, but there's a lot wrong with staying wrong. To not bother to correct a contradiction is a form of moral and intellectual suicide.

A couple with disparate views on marriage are going to have a rocky go of it. If the man thinks a good marriage includes other women but the wife disagrees, eventually there's going to be a serious problem, right? If I think that government exists to play "referee" - that is, to call fouls only and enforce the law without bias - but you think it exists to help "play the game", we have the same issue that the aforementioned husband and wife do. There's an irreconcilable difference in the fundamentals. If I think both Steph Curry and Joe Nobody deserve the same treatment from the refs, you'll call that unfair. If I believe it's none of my business that Steph is a once-in-a-lifetime shooter and Joe stinks, you'll demand that the refs change the game so that Joe's lack of talent is compensated.

You see, we can't discuss anything without resting our thoughts upon a theory. One's theory directs their practice. All practice is the practice of a theory. This is why it's so important to start our reasoning upon the correct foundation.

This is in evidence in the modern Wing Chun understanding of the term "bridge." Most understand it merely as a mechanical connection between two opponents. According to this theory, chi-sao is the ultimate bridge. Though we don't deny that this is, indeed, a "type" of bridge - limiting ourselves to it alone has had catastrophic consequences for the method. This flawed theory has led to the dreaded "Frankenchun monster" approach to combat...a fighter with dead footwork, standing straight up and in front of the enemy, marching stupidly into a set opponent.

It's the purely physical interpretation of the bridge concept that has led Wing Chun fighters to such serious tactical blunders. They stand straight in front of their enemy. They march straight in, exposing themselves to the full fury of their mobilized opponent. Modern Wing Chun fighters are, in this way, somewhat like the poor saps who rushed into gunfire during the Boxer's Rebellion. Yeah, the bullets killed those deluded souls who believed the nonsensical "experts" of their day, so it's not the same. But some of the epic beatdowns of Wing Chun fighters that we've all witnessed on YouTube have certainly slaughtered the confidence of many. Watching a fella stand straight in front of a guy, hands extended in the classic Wing Chun guard as if that alone will carry him to victory, and then getting bashed by overhands and hooks, or slammed to the ground from a double-leg, has become something like a violent Hallmark movie.

Predictable.

But if you've been told that Wing Chun is a "bridge art" and that statement has the full weight and trust of history behind it, who are you to doubt? And at first glance it makes sense. Bridging is certainly chi-sao and lop-sao drills. The problem is that seeing the bridging concept as the Art of War is like thinking you can put the ocean into a beach bucket. Chi-sao and other related drills are ways of training specific application reflexes of the bridge concept. They aren't to be confused with the concept itself. When we do that we see such desultory sights like we've witnessed on YouTube so many times. And maybe, just maybe, you've experienced that yourself.

But what is the bridge concept? That's the question we should be asking. The answer is found in Sun Tzu's classic. But to uncover it we must look at it with a fresh perspective. We must take off the modern shades, full of the pretty roses of modern life - its Starbucks and leisure - and see warfare as it is. We must also reject our modern bias about fighting. We see MMA and boxing as fighting. Yes, they are types of fighting but they aren't personal warfare and self-defense is personal war. If Russia and China battle, that's rightly considered as a war. When nations engage in kinetic conflict, it's a war. A large one. When individuals do the same thing, it's a small war. Thus, a martial art, true to its name, is a personal warfare system. This is what it means to say that you, a Wing Chun man/woman, are a warrior. You study the arts of personal warfare and prepare your body (the troops) to defeat an enemy using logical tactics (your mind is the general and officers).

A common misunderstanding of the Art of War is that Sun Tzu favored victory without fighting more than the actual defeat of his enemy. The problem with this interpretation is that he would've been talking about the *Art of Diplomacy* in that event, not war. Our modern sensitivities distort reality. We live in a very sissified age where people who disagree with us are considered guilty of violating our "safe space." That's ignoring, of course, Emerson's admonition to "...never fall into the vulgar mistake of dreaming that I am persecuted whenever I am contradicted." On the other hand, perhaps in reaction to this, some have embraced a hyper-aggressive "Cobra Kai" approach to training. I knew an instructor who was a veritable man-child, flying into a rage over the slightest provocation, self-indulgent, prone to screaming at students. His classes were, first and foremost, focused on preparation for competition. Predictably, his injury rates in training were similar to the driving record of teenage boys. His was the flip side of the coin of bad theory. Not wanting to be a wuss who talked about safe spaces, he and his students embraced an equally irrational but aggressive opposite approach, thereby being a poster child for the *either-or* fallacy.

What Sun Tzu was seeking was victory without a pitched battle. It wasn't an abhorrence of violence but a reticence to send your troops into a reckless fight. This is the idea. It's the study and practice of winning in the most efficient means possible.

Seeking the Bridge, therefore, isn't a matter of clinching or contact control alone, though it may at times include that. On the contrary, it means using tactics and technique in coordination with each other to control the enemy. Bridge control is dominance of position and timing. It may very well include control of their arms but that only happens (consistently and safely) through the use of the broader bridge concept.

What's instructive to know about the Art of War is that the whole bridge thing should be understood more directly than it often is. Sun Tzu was likely influenced by the battle between the Zu's and Han's. The Prince of Song's reticence to attack the larger army before it could get in formation caused his defeat. As it went, he was advised, due to the numerical superiority of the enemy, to attack as they crossed the bridge. He declined. Then he was urged to attack after they had crossed but still hadn't gotten into formation. We could see this as a "Jeet", that is, an interception of the enemy. Again, the Prince of Song declined. His reasoning is instructive.

To their urgent requests to fight the enemy while it was still weak, he said that one should "not attack the gray hair" nor "wound an enemy twice." In other words, he counted chivalry and a martial code as the basis for his poor tactical judgment. His generals replied, in effect, "why not send an army of aged fighters if that's the case?" They thought that the purpose of warfare was victory. They rightly saw it as the discipline of avoiding defeat by an attacker. A moral code that guaranteed defeat in war was an illogical one, they rightly argued. Unfazed, the Prince of Song led his men in battle only after the enemy was fully warmed up, so to speak.

And then they got trounced.

The lesson is that we should never fight Mike Tyson after he's warmed up and in the ring. Hit him with a brick during his ring walk. Sneak into his room and smother him when he's sleeping. Or get a time machine and go back to when he was a baby...

You get the idea.

Thus, the main theme of Art of War isn't avoiding confrontation but avoiding a pitched battle where it's all or nothing. An all or nothing campaign, even when you have a very good fighting force, is grotesquely destructive and ought to be avoided by any general with good sense. Why? Because it allows the opponent to fight at their best. It assures the greatest loss of men and material. This is the idea behind the *Jeet* and fighting "from the bridge" - it's the larger strategic order that puts one's tactics into context. Avoid a pitched battle! Technique is subservient to this goal just as the bridge concept is subservient to the goal of self-defense.

Again: avoid a pitched battle.

Fans love seeing "a good fight" because it's entertaining for block-heads the world over to watch other people get hurt. Tactical precision and good defense are far less popular among fans than, say, reckless aggression. But think for a second: if one's self-defense mirrors the tactical ethos of combat entertainment it violates the foundational goal, which is to keep oneself as safe as possible. Remember, being wrong isn't the problem; staying wrong is.

Thus, the smart warrior, the man/woman of intellect, discipline, skill, and moral courage, applies their mind to the battle. The mind is the highest weapon. Only fools rush into a fight, failing to seek tactical high-ground. The master trains for advantage...for the "edge".

Genghis Khan was an expert at this. So was Patton. They sought to use speed and mobility to make sure the enemy was at a disadvantage and so that their own troops were fighting from a tactical position that minimized their risk. All their mental efforts were focused on gaining such a tactical superiority that the enemy was at their weakest. George Washington did this at Trenton and Princeton. The crossing of the Delaware on Christmas night was exactly what Sun Tzu was talking about. Earlier in that same year, however, Washington and the Continental Army absorbed a colossal beating in New York. Why? Because they fought the superior British from a set position and the world's greatest navy was able to set up Washington's supposedly fortified positions for a thorough pounding. The Battle of New York in America's *War for Independence* was a one-sided beatdown that almost cost Washington the war. He learned his lesson.

Don't fight your enemy's strengths. Fight his weaknesses. That's the Art of War. That's the *bridge* we seek to fight from. The reason many people can't make sense of fighting from the bridge in the wooden sense of the term is because it doesn't make any sense. It sets us up for failure by assuming an unrealistic fighting reality. In other words, the ubiquitous misconception of fighting from the bridge is erroneous and, therefore, tactically stupid exactly because it isn't tactical.

Logical Wing Chun is, therefore, built upon this strategic foundation. To not fight his weaknesses is to allow the enemy a Prince of Song moment. His army lost and he died. When Mao was criticized for his tactics in China he once replied, *"Am I the Prince of Song?"* Now, clearly, I'm not arguing that Mao was a moral warrior. He was a monster. But monsters and tyrants, if they're effective at all, must and will use sound strategy.

Think about Hitler and his downfall for a moment.

His blitzkrieg attacks gave him all of Europe. The speed and precision of his army overwhelmed the continent and by June of 1941 he had no threats whatsoever. But then he decided to attack his buddy to the East, Joseph Stalin. And he was winning quite handily until he made the fatal blunder of going after Stalingrad on the way to securing oil in Crimea. Why go after Stalingrad at all? It made no tactical sense and drew that swift and destructive German army into a slugfest. Stalingrad became a "rat-war" waged amidst the brutal cold and crumbled ruins of the bombed-out city. It was like Floyd Mayweather digging in his heels and brawling. Why would a great boxer, untouched and undefeated, give up his long game and go in the trenches?

And that's the way Hitler lost World War Two.

If Hitler had studied Sun Tzu and the lessons of the Prince of Song (or even reckoned with what happened to Napoleon) he might have avoided that whole ignominious honeymoon/suicide thing he had with Eva Braun. Likewise, if we want to get the most of our beloved art, and avoid similar shellackings, we must reckon with the strategic and tactical implications of Chum Kiu. The "bridge seeking form" is telling us much more than we think. Chum Kiu is telling us to study and apply the principles of Art of War.

Another important aspect to consider, once we comprehend this, is that we'll stop trying to do combative things that "look like Wing Chun" (i.e., do things that look like classroom drills) and focus instead on tactical issues. Fighting to the enemy's weakness to "secure the bridge" is the key. We must be trained, body and mind, to think and fight this way. We must be trained to understand the critical difference between sparring drills, chi-sao, and actual fighting in the same way that soldiers recognize that combat is different than marching.